the Looking Glass

GLIMPSES OF LIFE THROUGH POETRY

BY LISA SHERK

Illustrated by
Megan Harrisson

Dedication

"One beautiful heart is better
than a thousand beautiful faces"

– William Shakespeare

I dedicate this book to all the people I love most in this life: my mom, Irene; son Jacob and daughter Tessa, both of whom I am so incredibly proud of; grandchildren Cailee, Beau, and Oak; and my beautiful Erv. Thank you to my dearest and best friends Barbara and Connie, who have been my loyal and most loving companions. You have always been my people, my rock, my biggest supporters, and my hands to hold.

And thank you to Nancy, who encouraged me and assisted me with this project.

I will forever be grateful.

 FriesenPress

One Printers Way
Altona, MB R0G 0B0
Canada

www.friesenpress.com

Copyright © 2022 by Lisa Sherk, CC RN
Illustrator, Megan Harrisson
First Edition — 2022

ISBN
978-1-03-915939-6 (Hardcover)
978-1-03-915938-9 (Paperback)
978-1-03-915940-2 (eBook)

1. POETRY, SUBJECTS & THEMES, INSPIRATION & RELIGIOUS

Distributed to the trade by The Ingram Book Company

Table of Contents

the Looking glass

The Looking Glass

As I peer through the glass
of this life I have led
mountains and valleys
narrowest threads

Doors closed, disappointments,
dreams obscured, afraid to leap,
secrets and hopes
in this heart that I keep

Such moments of delight
full of family and friends
laughter, celebrations,
days full of intent

In a moment it seems
I have blinked, years sped by
My children, now grown
like bluebirds that fly

into beautiful people
I'm proud they are mine
my greatest treasures
none other I'll find

I reflect and remember
a much younger self
pull out aspirations
tucked deep on a shelf

Although lines on my face
grey hair on my head
a stirring peeks forth
It's your time, a voice says

My hand races forth
across paper with pen
my dreams come to life
with the stories I tend

The looking glass opens
of life moving forth
sunshine filters through
hope is the source

More stories are woven
a tapestry made
filaments of my lifetime
across the white page

Visions take on shapes
have voices at last
come along with me
peer. . .through the looking glass

Beachglass Girl

A beachglass girl throws
on her boots

searches the shore for
glass that floats

it winks and sparkles
at the water's edge

glistens blue, green,
purple, red

broken pottery pieces
that tell a story

of ages past in all
its glory

waves do crash
they ebb and flow

sand and water
feed her soul

a beachglass girl
meets other friends

that search, explore,
replenish, extend

welcoming smiles,
understanding nods

of countless searches
a beachwalk trod

So for today,
glass and sand

wash over her soul
like a soothing hand

God's beauty; its splendour
on this beach she loves

whispered prayers of
thanks sent above

Beachglass girl.

The Beachwalker

She zips her coat
pulls up her hood
steps outside
as emotions flood

There's brokenness
vacant spaces
where once was love
emptiness she faces

Winds blow strong
whip her hair about
waves are crashing in
seagulls shout

She lets the sand
and waves bring healing
washing over her with
comforting feelings

She hears God's voice
in the lapping waves
it gives her peace
like a balm that saves

Her strength and courage
will carry her
through the drifting motion
of the beach's lure

She lifts her face
feels the sunshine's warmth
rests sure and calm,
God knows her storms

She sees His hand
in the glistening stones
the water smoothes
she is not alone

With each step she takes
in the warm, lush sand
goes the beach walker
a resilient woman

God Is. . .

God is the One who I cling to
when the winds are fierce

The hand that I hold
the dryer of tears

God is the maker of
each tiny bird that sings

He's created each fluttering
butterfly wing

God is the balm to a soul
that is broken and bruised

The maker of rainbows
in beautiful hues

God is the creator
of each crashing wave in the sea

The maker of mountains
the giver of dreams

God is Alpha–Omega
beginning and end

My loving Saviour
my dearest friend

God is the giver of peace
the mender of hearts

He is the grace deliverer
He creates brand new starts

There are not enough words
to describe who God is

All I know for sure
He is mine; I am His.

God is ...

God Speaks

God speaks to me
in this old beach chair
as I gaze out upon
waves that crash and flare

Rolling in with the waves
meditation resides
rooted low in my soul
covers hurt submerged inside

When we take time alone
oh, such beauty compounds
as I hear thunderous winds
a cacophony of sounds

Yet the sun winks through
midst a large white cloud
much like peace in my soul
joy proliferates out loud

Hope crescendos like a song
after nature's long drought
glimpse the fluttering wing
as the seagulls shout

I'm sure that God speaks
through all He creates
if we take time, let go
all our worries abate

Roll out like the tide
as if polished beachglass
our edges are smoothed
from life's trials that pass

I'll be still, close my eyes
hear the sounds of the waves
fathomless in my chair
gratitude for today

Know that God speaks
to a soul that is open
lift up your heart's window
whispered prayers
revered,
spoken

The Piano

She sits down gently
on the old, wooden bench
placed beautifully in front
of the piano she tends

Her fingers start to dance
across the keys, black and white
her heart begins to sing
words inside her give respite

Music calms an ache
in her soul
she feels it lift
an embroidered piece that's woven
like the sands,
o'er rocks that sift

Her voice begins to rise
like the waves on ocean's shores
her spirits lift
like eagle's wings,
like rain that gently pours

That is music's gift that flows
from the piano she plays,
takes away the agonies
from all her yesterdays

Gives her hope and heals
broken crevices like glue

her piano stands

embraces her

she plays

music soothes

the Piano

A Mother Is

A mother is a holder of hands

who gets us through life's sinking sands

A mother is a dryer of tears

the one who calms, and eases our fears

A mother is a memory keeper

a listening ear, a wisdom seeker

A mother is a Godly example

following His word, giving

scripture to sample

A mother is a cookie baker

a party planner, a meal maker

A mother is a secret keeper

our biggest cheerleader, a dream seeker

But most of all a mother is

a woman who knows

we are His

She is here to pray, guide, love

gain her wisdom from above

She is the one

placed here on earth

who loves you more

believes your worth

a mother is...

A Lovely Day

You race down the steps
from your sunroom that's bright

throw open the door
your brown eyes pure light

You start to describe
the week you have had

I listen and smile
knowing my heart is clad

with joy and such love
I'm so proud of this girl

who is strong, courageous,
intelligent, pure

My daughter whose beauty
goes beyond the outside

her laughter and humour,
qualities that reside

We sit in a bookshop
sipping our cappuccinos

browse through books
on the bookshelves,
love of reading and vino

Then to the antique shop
with wares on display

all of the while
enjoying a lovely day

The sun shines
such beauty,
and your eyes
they sparkle

I relish and marvel
my daughter,
a wonder

Enjoying each minute
hand in hand
all the way,

immersed in the beauty
of this lovely day

The Garden

The garden is a place to gaze
upon God's glorious summer days

a place of rest,
an oasis transformed

forgotten snow,
summer's warmth
a cardinal perched on a willow branch,

rustling leaves
evening dance

sounds of cicadas
nature's stereo

on this porch swing I rest
paradise overflows

as I ponder, the garden
is much like life

full of dirt and weeds,
rocks, and strife

with love, patience,
faith, strength

emerges beauty, healing
like nature's rain

for today, God's beauty astounds
amongst trees and flowers
planted in the ground

of this little garden
I look upon

buoyant hope,
my heart sings a birdsong

the garden

The Garden Shoes

The door swings open

in the early morn

as the sun shines in

through a heart forlorn

a veil of grief

runs wide and deep

down a lined, worn face

brown eyes that weep

She slips on his shoes

resting by the door

hears the creaking sound

of the cottage floor

looks through the panes

of the windows past

to the garden planted

by her brother's hands

Her feet start to tread

in the garden shoes

Her spirits lift

from the shining hues

of the flower's beauty

planted out of love

Hydrangeas, lilies, and foxglove

pacify her soul

fill her heart with joy

as the sun shines brilliantly

her thoughts of that boy

Memories flood

of a lifetime spent

with such love and laughter

that came and went

she slides on his shoes

that are far too big

yet, they fit perfectly

as she's remembering. . .

the garden shoes

Grief

Grief came knocking at my door
I let the pain seep from my pores

hand in hand
this grief and I,
sat silently as memories fly

across the screen of my lifetime
pictures of you,
they all are mine

I cherish every moment, day
you were in
why can't you stay?

rather, grief sits silently
beside this chair
there's only me

we embrace
tears run down,
this creased, worn face
sadness so profound

all I know
I have to open
the door of grief,
mend a heart that's broken

like an old, worn shawl
thrown over me,
I hold grief's hand
with time, pain flees

in its place
tucked in my heart,
are memories that
will ne'er depart

like the cavernous ocean
full of my tears
are moments, a lifetime
all the years

I had with you
what a gift that was,
to have had the treasure
of your love

So for today
as grief came knocking,
an opened door
grief and I sat talking

I let the pain
wash over me,
knowing down the road
comes a full healing

we'll sit side by side
on this chair
grief and I

look out frosted windows
at the grey winter sky

embrace quietly
let the memories flood

of a million moments
my heart bursts with love

I will rest,
feel such peace
God and I will be talking

I will open the door
when grief comes knocking

grief.

All the Corners of My Heart

I close my eyes
start to pull
memories
they overflow

rarest gems
rubies, emerald, gold
tucked recollected
a treasure trove

in all the corners
of my heart
such beauty, magic,
a singing lark

are there to pull
at any moment
from the treasure chest
like an ocean flowing

though you're gone,
you can't be seen
I hear and feel
memories

laughter, smiles,
your voice that speaks,
love I felt
only you could reach

I bask in the beauty
anytime,
although you're gone
memories are mine

in all the corners
of my heart
I hear you, feel you
always will be part

of every fibre
that is me
echoes, voices,
memories

to wrap around
my broken heart
spinning, twirling
like a ballerina skirt

as I sit alone
or in a crowd,
hearing your voice
I make you proud

fly away
heaven in your reach,
flutter angel wings
lessons you will teach

though my tears
flow free
fill a large
ship's port

you are there,
tucked
in all the corners
of my heart

the
Memory quilt

The Memory Quilt

Tattered linens
coloured thread
sewn together
thoughts unsaid

her eyes closed tightly
visions appear
of years before
she lets the tears

flow free, so softly
not wiped away
rather feelings raw
echoes stay

the memory quilt
lies on her shoulders
each piece of fabric
like arms that hold her

materials pieced
her brother's clothes
now stitched together
as the needle sews

so many stories
fondly remembered
a lifetime lived
like a fire's embers

the quilt rests lightly
wrapped 'round her arms
she feels him still
a smile forms

peace engulfs her
the memory quilt
lies soft, so gently
feels her heart fill

what a gift was given
fabric, needle, thread
the worn soft blanket
she bows her head

thankful every moment
she had his love
closes tear-soaked eyes
lets the memories flood

Rain

In the early morn
an October rain

falls down like droplets
on the windowpane

glistens like a diamond
of the finest ring

sounds of nature's music
a robin sings

the gentle hum
raindrops' drumming sounds

such serene feelings
can be found

in God's voice that speaks
through all He made

as we stop and listen
nature's symphony creates

such glorious music
thunderous, crashing sounds

lightning flashes, thus
happiness is found

my heart beats softly
peace o'erflows

with the sounds of raindrops
lie my worries, woes

rest for the moment
sounds of gentle rain

falling sure and steady
on the windowpane

knowing much like life
after thunderstorms

the sun bursts through
in its place such warmth

on this rainy morning
an October day

I will cherish raindrops
nature's healing ways

rest in the moment
all as it should be

peer through the window
raindrops all I see

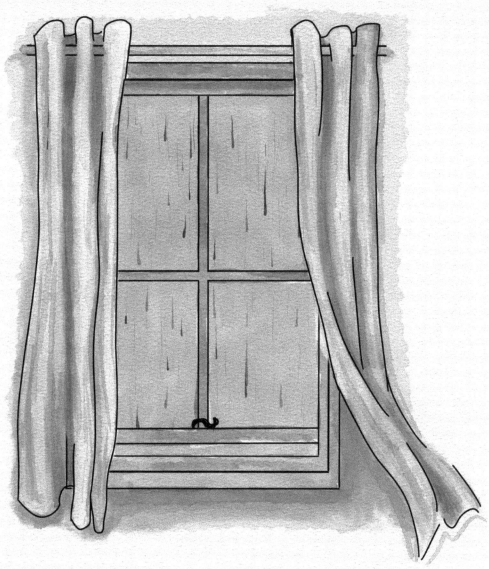

The Whippoorwill

There's a bird
that sings
when the air
has a chill,
the sun disappears
as the darkness fills,
the night sky
with stars
ever twinkling but still,
the intense, sharp call
of the whippoorwill
often deep in the shadows
of my life
I have heard,
God speak
clearly to me
like these nocturnal birds,
a whispered voice
often signs
can be seen,
when we still
our thoughts
take time peacefully
it's in tranquil places
with our eyes closed
at rest,
nature's beauty overflows
like the whippoorwill's nest,
piercing calls auscultate
slice through air
loud and pure,
answers often make a sound

problems no longer blurred,
amidst uncertainty, unknown
there is One
who's in control,
much like honey that trickles
from a bee's honeycomb,
use your voice
sing at will,
never wavering
be still,
when it's darkest
through the clouds
be the whippoorwill

Whippoorwill

The Mooring

Like a ship secured
by an anchor
made of steel

forever resolute
against bitter winds
you feel

there are times
to abide
often shielded
strength revealed

steadfast in the harbour
ever faithful
knees that kneel

moorings in my life
always constant,
ardent, sure

mother, dearest friends,
daughter,
love, flawless pure

amidst the storms
that rage
lightning flashes
rains that pour

God has placed
all I need
these strong women
who endure

lessons
I have learned
answers given in the lull

amongst the quiet
hush of silence
there I hear
the Master's call

His voice soothes
all my fears
of the answers, yet unseen

assuaging the uncertainties
worries, lessening

like the ship
that's battered
by the waters'
waves and winds

be relentless,
ever strengthened,
undisturbed,
a firm, tree limb

know God is
beside you

has the answers
listening

an anchor,

unobscured,

my strength,

the mooring

the
Mooring

Winter Walk

Heavy coat
woollen mittens
crunching snow
midst these leaden boots,
snowflakes swirling
crisp air falls fresh
on my cheeks
like a butterfly's
wing that floats,
branches laden
with heavy snow,
laughter heard
on the lake below
as the blades
of the skates
slice through the air,
unbridled joy
not a worry or care,
nature's playground awaits
on my winter walk
trudging on,
lift my head,
nod hello,
see the flock
of the geese
as they waddle
on icy paths,
a cardinal perched
on a snowy branch
such marvel flourishes
God's beauty outdoors,
as the wind blows

snow flies,
chills me deep
to the core
I reflect how the winter
can mimic my life,
has seen storms
gales blowing
cuts deep, like a knife
yet after the thaw
of a cold winter's night
comes the warmth
and bright sunshine
God's promise
takes flight,
I know
He's heard me
dried all my tears,
held my hand
through the blustery
winter years
so today
as I trudge
on these wide
winter paths,
I shall lift up my face
shimmering rays
I will bask,
cradle the joy
that's been given
it's free,
feel the fathomless
sunshine
nestled deep
within me

Winter
Walk

Second Chances

This life that I've led
mistakes I have made
often narrow,
crooked paths
full of memories
that fade

dreams lay dormant
buried beneath
like the blowing
winter snow

a hopeful heart
beats strong
in this chest
that I know

an awakening
peeks forth
in a life
that's seen such storms

second chances
are held
like a dress
that adorns

full of beauty
and hope
shimmers like
sun on sea

suddenly,
I'm sure
God's plans
navigate in me

this heart
that is fractured
starts to heal
with love's glue

vacant spaces
and rooms
fully filled
with oceans blue

I know
at last I'm home
nestled deep
beside a soul

who has mended
fissured pieces,
made your heart
my home

whispered prayers of thanks
like dances,
from a girl
who prayed, believed

thankful,
every minute, day
for a life
of second chances

Second
chances

The List

A journal opened
the white page fresh
with words unspoken
now written in pen
her hidden yearnings
locked deep in a vault
a jar full of her tears
the sharp taste of salt
are wiped away quickly
she feverishly writes
qualities, hopes,
dreams come to life
one word after another
the list takes on form
a love she has searched for
lies in reach evermore
selfless, kind,
full of laughter,
loves to travel, explore,
holds my hand
adores me
books strewn
on the wood floor
in the morning
hot coffee,
side by side,
smiling eyes
the list I had written
is at last
fully sized
before me I gaze
at my partner

best friend
a lover of family
such a gift
has been sent
my cup runneth over
elation overflows
tattered list
tucked, remembered
full of faith
that she knows
simplest of hopes
each day
she is kissed
all her prayers
God has answered
piece of paper
the list

A Thousand Lifetimes

Until the sun in the sky
    decides not to shine
rivers and oceans
    they all run dry
'til the birds in the air
    no longer fly
I will love you for a
    thousand, a thousand lifetimes

As we walk hand in hand
    dreams woven, sublime
'til my heart stops beating
    in this chest of mine
'til I'm old and grey
    with wrinkles 'round these hazel eyes
I will love you for a
    thousand, a thousand lifetimes

As the fabric of our lives
    untangles and winds
like a long country road
    it's a treasure we find
your beautiful heart
    beats and is mine
I will love you for a
    thousand, a thousand lifetimes

I will cherish this gift
    God has destined the signs
like your arms that hold
    me, forever entwined
I will tenderly hold
    your heart that is kind
I will love you for a
    thousand, a thousand lifetimes

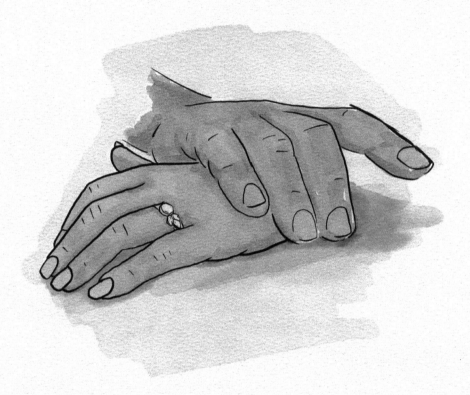

a thousand
lifetimes

Walnut Cottage

I round the bend
see the Lake Erie shore
turn down Walnut Street
view the home
I adore
nestled deep
on a lot
is a cottage
with stone
a cobblestone walk
where I'm never alone
contentment cascades
when I walk
through the door
throw open
the shutters
hear the waves
as they roar
on the porch swing
I rest
by the fire
that's warm
midst the blankets
pillows
red rug
on the floor
where visions
of laughter
piano, guitars,
my children
loved ones
surround me like stars

are brilliant, fluorescent
such beauty
that shines
because love
lives at Walnut
in this cottage
this time
where dreams
come to life
because chances
were taken
gone are tears
the sadness
fond memories
now making
it's never too late
to believe
there is more
dreams
can be grasped
to achieve
explore
you are never
too old
to reach
for the stars
find the rarest
of treasures
like beachglass
in jars
sun shines
through windows
of Walnut Cottage
warmth spreads
in my heart
pictures, collages
books stacked
in bookcases
music plays gently

all is
as it should be
in this place
God sent me

The Dreammaker

You walked through my door
pumpkin scones
in your hand

two shattered hearts
secured by thread,
rubber bands

you waited with patience
I let my heart open,
ever so slowly
healed all that was broken

long conversations
like hourglass sand,
walks in the forest
gently you took my hand

together we healed
such immeasurable hurt,
making a pathway
plans to go forth

the dreammaker appeared
never envisioned a man,
with every quality dreamt of
ever imagined

now here before me
a carpenter, pilot,
baker of pies,
history zealot

enthusiasm seeps
out of every pore,
together we forage
through antique and bookstores

dreaming, planning
heads thrown back as we're laughing,
a house on the beach
in the sunroom we're dancing

I'll climb every mountain
in valleys forsaken,
knowing all of its worth
the long road I've taken

the key to my heart
has been opened, awakened,
twenty years not enough
you and I, dreammaking

the
dreammaker

About the Author

Lisa Sherk lives in Port Colborne, Ontario, Canada and has been a critical care registered nurse in the Intensive Care Unit for thirty-six years. Her love of writing has endured since she was a young girl, and now her dreams of publishing her poetry have come to fruition. She has two beautiful children and three grandchildren. She lives with the love of her life Ervin. *The Looking Glass* is her story and glimpses of her life, through poetry.

About the Illustrator

Megan Harrisson has been painting and drawing since early childhood. Now a critical care registered nurse with a passion for both healthcare and the visual arts, she creates both personally inspired work and creative commissions utilizing paint on canvas, watercolour paint, linework, and digital design. This love for creativity and exploration of varying concepts, styles, and medium brings opportunity to align and understand others' perspectives and emotions to be translated into her artwork. Illustrations for these poems have been created through close collaboration to translate the emotions and feelings of the author, the reader, and those who have inspired the carefully stitched, heartfelt words.

CPSIA information can be obtained
at www.ICGtesting.com
Printed in the USA
BVHW020000171122
651992BV00001B/1

9 781039 159389